50 Classic Greek Dishes for Every Occasion

By: Kelly Johnson

Table of Contents

- Moussaka (Layered Eggplant and Meat Casserole)
- Souvlaki (Grilled Meat Skewers)
- Tzatziki (Yogurt and Cucumber Dip)
- Spanakopita (Spinach and Feta Pie)
- Greek Salad (Horiatiki)
- Dolmades (Stuffed Grape Leaves)
- Fasolada (Traditional Greek Bean Soup)
- Pastitsio (Greek Baked Pasta with Meat Sauce)
- Gigantes Plaki (Baked Giant Beans in Tomato Sauce)
- Kolokithokeftedes (Zucchini Fritters)
- Loukoumades (Greek Honey Puffs)
- Kleftiko (Slow-Roasted Lamb)
- Stifado (Greek Beef Stew with Onions)
- Youvetsi (Lamb or Beef with Orzo)
- Gemista (Stuffed Tomatoes and Peppers)
- Avgolemono Soup (Lemon Chicken and Rice Soup)
- Saganaki (Pan-Seared Greek Cheese)
- Skordalia (Garlic and Potato Dip)
- Baklava (Honey and Nut Phyllo Pastry)
- Briam (Greek Roasted Vegetables)
- Revithada (Greek Chickpea Stew)
- Koulouri (Sesame-Crusted Greek Bread Rings)
- Melitzanosalata (Smoky Eggplant Dip)
- Fava (Santorini Yellow Split Pea Puree)
- Taramosalata (Fish Roe Spread)
- Psari Plaki (Baked Fish with Tomatoes and Onions)
- Horta Vrasta (Boiled Wild Greens with Olive Oil and Lemon)
- Xtapodi Krasato (Braised Octopus in Wine)
- Lamb Fricassee with Avgolemono Sauce
- Halva (Semolina-Based Sweet Dessert)
- Rizogalo (Greek Rice Pudding)
- Kourabiedes (Powdered Sugar Butter Cookies)
- Kataifi (Shredded Phyllo Pastry with Nuts and Syrup)
- Bougatsa (Greek Custard-Filled Pastry)
- Loukaniko (Greek Sausage with Orange Zest)

- Soutzoukakia (Greek Meatballs in Tomato Sauce)
- Choriatiki Omeleta (Greek Village Omelet)
- Lagana (Greek Flatbread)
- Tsoureki (Greek Easter Bread)
- Pita Me Gyro (Greek Gyro Wrap)
- Sfakiani Pita (Cheese-Filled Cretan Pie with Honey)
- Kalamarakia Tiganita (Fried Calamari)
- Midia Saganaki (Mussels in Tomato and Feta Sauce)
- Amygdalota (Greek Almond Cookies)
- Spetsofai (Sausage and Peppers in Tomato Sauce)
- Hortopita (Wild Greens and Cheese Pie)
- Paximadia (Greek Twice-Baked Biscotti)
- Fasolakia Ladera (Braised Green Beans in Olive Oil)
- Marides Tiganites (Fried Whitebait Fish)
- Galaktoboureko (Greek Custard Pie with Syrup)

Moussaka (Layered Eggplant and Meat Casserole)

Ingredients:

- 2 large eggplants, sliced
- 1 lb ground beef or lamb
- 1 onion, diced
- 2 cloves garlic, minced
- 1 can diced tomatoes
- 1 teaspoon cinnamon
- ½ teaspoon oregano
- ½ teaspoon salt
- ½ teaspoon black pepper
- 1 cup béchamel sauce
- ¼ cup grated Parmesan cheese
- 2 tablespoons olive oil

Instructions:

1. Brush eggplant slices with olive oil and roast at 375°F (190°C) for 15 minutes.
2. Sauté onion and garlic, then add ground meat, tomatoes, and spices. Simmer for 15 minutes.
3. Layer eggplant and meat sauce in a baking dish, then top with béchamel and Parmesan.
4. Bake at 375°F (190°C) for 30 minutes.

Souvlaki (Grilled Meat Skewers)

Ingredients:

- 1 lb chicken or pork, cubed
- 2 tablespoons olive oil
- 1 tablespoon lemon juice
- 2 cloves garlic, minced
- 1 teaspoon oregano
- ½ teaspoon salt
- ½ teaspoon black pepper

Instructions:

1. Mix olive oil, lemon juice, garlic, oregano, salt, and pepper.
2. Marinate meat for at least 2 hours.
3. Thread onto skewers and grill for 10 minutes, turning occasionally.

Tzatziki (Yogurt and Cucumber Dip)

Ingredients:

- 1 cup Greek yogurt
- ½ cucumber, grated and drained
- 1 clove garlic, minced
- 1 tablespoon olive oil
- 1 teaspoon lemon juice
- 1 teaspoon dill
- Salt and pepper to taste

Instructions:

1. Mix all ingredients in a bowl.
2. Chill for at least 30 minutes before serving.

Spanakopita (Spinach and Feta Pie)

Ingredients:

- 1 lb spinach, chopped
- 1 small onion, diced
- 2 cloves garlic, minced
- 1 cup feta cheese, crumbled
- 2 eggs, beaten
- 1 teaspoon dill
- ½ teaspoon black pepper
- 8 sheets phyllo dough
- ¼ cup melted butter

Instructions:

1. Sauté onion, garlic, and spinach until wilted.
2. Mix with feta, eggs, dill, and pepper.
3. Layer phyllo dough, brushing each sheet with butter.
4. Add filling, top with more phyllo, and bake at 375°F (190°C) for 30 minutes.

Greek Salad (Horiatiki)

Ingredients:

- 2 tomatoes, chopped
- 1 cucumber, sliced
- ½ red onion, sliced
- ½ cup Kalamata olives
- ¼ cup feta cheese, cubed
- 1 tablespoon olive oil
- 1 teaspoon oregano
- Salt and pepper to taste

Instructions:

1. Toss all ingredients in a bowl.
2. Drizzle with olive oil and sprinkle with oregano.

Dolmades (Stuffed Grape Leaves)

Ingredients:

- 20 grape leaves, rinsed
- ½ cup cooked rice
- ½ cup ground beef or lamb (optional)
- 1 small onion, minced
- 1 teaspoon allspice
- ½ teaspoon cinnamon
- ½ teaspoon salt
- 1 tablespoon lemon juice

Instructions:

1. Mix rice, meat (if using), onion, spices, and lemon juice.
2. Place 1 teaspoon of filling in each grape leaf and roll tightly.
3. Place in a pot, cover with water, and simmer for 40 minutes.

Fasolada (Traditional Greek Bean Soup)

Ingredients:

- 1 can white beans, drained
- 1 onion, diced
- 2 carrots, sliced
- 2 cloves garlic, minced
- 1 can diced tomatoes
- 4 cups vegetable broth
- 1 teaspoon oregano
- 1 tablespoon olive oil
- Salt and pepper to taste

Instructions:

1. Sauté onion, garlic, and carrots in olive oil.
2. Add beans, tomatoes, broth, oregano, salt, and pepper.
3. Simmer for 30 minutes before serving.

Pastitsio (Greek Baked Pasta with Meat Sauce)

Ingredients:

- 8 oz penne pasta
- 1 lb ground beef or lamb
- 1 onion, diced
- 2 cloves garlic, minced
- 1 can tomato sauce
- 1 teaspoon cinnamon
- ½ teaspoon nutmeg
- 1 cup béchamel sauce
- ¼ cup grated Parmesan cheese

Instructions:

1. Cook pasta according to package instructions.
2. Sauté onion, garlic, and meat, then add tomato sauce and spices. Simmer for 15 minutes.
3. Layer pasta, meat sauce, and béchamel in a baking dish.
4. Top with Parmesan and bake at 375°F (190°C) for 30 minutes.

Gigantes Plaki (Baked Giant Beans in Tomato Sauce)

Ingredients:

- 1 can giant beans (or butter beans), drained
- 1 can diced tomatoes
- 1 small onion, diced
- 2 cloves garlic, minced
- 1 teaspoon oregano
- 1 tablespoon olive oil
- Salt and pepper to taste

Instructions:

1. Sauté onion and garlic in olive oil.
2. Add tomatoes, oregano, salt, and pepper. Simmer for 10 minutes.
3. Stir in beans and bake at 375°F (190°C) for 20 minutes.

Kolokithokeftedes (Zucchini Fritters)

Ingredients:

- 2 zucchinis, grated and drained
- ½ cup feta cheese, crumbled
- ¼ cup breadcrumbs
- 1 egg
- 1 teaspoon dill
- ½ teaspoon black pepper
- Olive oil for frying

Instructions:

1. Mix zucchini, feta, breadcrumbs, egg, dill, and pepper.
2. Form into small patties and fry in olive oil until golden brown.

Loukoumades (Greek Honey Puffs)

Ingredients:

- 1 cup flour
- 1 teaspoon yeast
- ½ cup warm water
- 1 tablespoon sugar
- ½ teaspoon salt
- 1 tablespoon honey
- ¼ teaspoon cinnamon
- Oil for frying

Instructions:

1. Mix flour, yeast, water, sugar, and salt into a batter. Let rise for 1 hour.
2. Drop spoonfuls into hot oil and fry until golden.
3. Drizzle with honey and sprinkle with cinnamon.

Kleftiko (Slow-Roasted Lamb)

Ingredients:

- 2 lbs lamb shoulder
- 2 tablespoons olive oil
- 4 cloves garlic, minced
- 1 teaspoon oregano
- 1 teaspoon rosemary
- 1 teaspoon salt
- ½ teaspoon black pepper
- 2 potatoes, chopped
- Juice of 1 lemon

Instructions:

1. Rub lamb with olive oil, garlic, oregano, rosemary, salt, and pepper.
2. Place in a roasting dish with potatoes and lemon juice.
3. Cover and bake at 325°F (160°C) for 3 hours.

Stifado (Greek Beef Stew with Onions)

Ingredients:

- 1 ½ lbs beef, cubed
- 1 lb pearl onions, peeled
- 2 tablespoons olive oil
- 2 cloves garlic, minced
- 1 can diced tomatoes
- 1 cup red wine
- 1 cinnamon stick
- 1 teaspoon allspice
- 1 teaspoon oregano
- Salt and pepper to taste

Instructions:

1. Heat olive oil in a pot and brown the beef. Remove and set aside.
2. Sauté onions and garlic until fragrant.
3. Return beef to the pot and add tomatoes, wine, cinnamon, allspice, oregano, salt, and pepper.
4. Simmer for 1.5–2 hours until tender.

Youvetsi (Lamb or Beef with Orzo)

Ingredients:

- 1 ½ lbs lamb or beef, cubed
- 1 cup orzo pasta
- 1 onion, diced
- 2 cloves garlic, minced
- 1 can diced tomatoes
- 1 teaspoon cinnamon
- 1 teaspoon oregano
- 2 cups beef broth
- ¼ cup grated Kefalotyri or Parmesan cheese
- 2 tablespoons olive oil

Instructions:

1. Heat olive oil in a pot and brown meat.
2. Add onion, garlic, tomatoes, cinnamon, oregano, and broth. Simmer for 1 hour.
3. Stir in orzo and cook for 10 minutes until tender.
4. Sprinkle with cheese before serving.

Gemista (Stuffed Tomatoes and Peppers)

Ingredients:

- 4 large tomatoes
- 4 bell peppers
- 1 cup rice
- ½ cup ground beef (optional)
- 1 small onion, diced
- 2 cloves garlic, minced
- 1 teaspoon oregano
- ½ teaspoon cinnamon
- 2 tablespoons olive oil
- Salt and pepper to taste

Instructions:

1. Cut off tops of tomatoes and peppers, remove seeds and pulp.
2. Sauté onion, garlic, rice, beef (if using), and seasonings in olive oil.
3. Fill tomatoes and peppers with mixture, replace tops.
4. Bake at 375°F (190°C) for 45 minutes.

Avgolemono Soup (Lemon Chicken and Rice Soup)

Ingredients:

- 1 lb chicken breast
- 6 cups chicken broth
- ½ cup rice
- 2 eggs
- Juice of 2 lemons
- Salt and pepper to taste

Instructions:

1. Cook chicken in broth, then shred.
2. Add rice to broth and cook until tender.
3. Whisk eggs and lemon juice in a bowl.
4. Slowly add hot broth to egg mixture, then return to the pot.
5. Stir in chicken and season with salt and pepper.

Saganaki (Pan-Seared Greek Cheese)

Ingredients:

- 1 block Kefalotyri or Halloumi cheese
- 2 tablespoons flour
- 2 tablespoons olive oil
- 1 lemon, cut into wedges

Instructions:

1. Coat cheese lightly with flour.
2. Heat olive oil in a pan and fry cheese until golden brown on both sides.
3. Serve immediately with lemon wedges.

Skordalia (Garlic and Potato Dip)

Ingredients:

- 2 large potatoes, boiled
- 4 cloves garlic, minced
- ¼ cup olive oil
- 2 tablespoons lemon juice
- Salt to taste

Instructions:

1. Mash potatoes with garlic, olive oil, lemon juice, and salt until smooth.

Baklava (Honey and Nut Phyllo Pastry)

Ingredients:

- 1 package phyllo dough
- 1 cup walnuts, chopped
- 1 cup almonds, chopped
- ½ teaspoon cinnamon
- ½ cup melted butter
- ½ cup honey
- ½ teaspoon vanilla extract

Instructions:

1. Layer phyllo dough, brushing each layer with butter.
2. Mix nuts and cinnamon, spread over phyllo layers.
3. Repeat layering, then bake at 350°F (175°C) for 35 minutes.
4. Drizzle with honey and vanilla while warm.

Briam (Greek Roasted Vegetables)

Ingredients:

- 1 zucchini, sliced
- 1 eggplant, cubed
- 2 potatoes, sliced
- 1 bell pepper, chopped
- 1 can diced tomatoes
- 2 cloves garlic, minced
- 2 tablespoons olive oil
- 1 teaspoon oregano
- Salt and pepper to taste

Instructions:

1. Toss all ingredients in a baking dish.
2. Bake at 400°F (200°C) for 45 minutes, stirring halfway.

Revithada (Greek Chickpea Stew)

Ingredients:

- 2 cups cooked chickpeas
- 1 small onion, diced
- 2 cloves garlic, minced
- 1 teaspoon oregano
- ½ teaspoon cumin
- 1 tablespoon olive oil
- 4 cups vegetable broth

Instructions:

1. Sauté onion and garlic in olive oil.
2. Add chickpeas, broth, oregano, and cumin.
3. Simmer for 30 minutes.

Koulouri (Sesame-Crusted Greek Bread Rings)

Ingredients:

- 3 cups all-purpose flour
- 1 teaspoon sugar
- 1 teaspoon salt
- 1 teaspoon yeast
- 1 cup warm water
- ½ cup sesame seeds

Instructions:

1. Mix flour, sugar, salt, yeast, and warm water to form dough. Let rise for 1 hour.
2. Shape into rings, brush with water, and coat with sesame seeds.
3. Bake at 375°F (190°C) for 20 minutes.

Melitzanosalata (Smoky Eggplant Dip)

Ingredients:

- 2 large eggplants
- 2 cloves garlic, minced
- 2 tablespoons olive oil
- 1 tablespoon lemon juice
- ½ teaspoon salt
- 1 tablespoon chopped parsley

Instructions:

1. Roast eggplants at 400°F (200°C) for 40 minutes until soft.
2. Scoop out flesh and mash with garlic, olive oil, lemon juice, and salt.
3. Garnish with parsley before serving.

Fava (Santorini Yellow Split Pea Puree)

Ingredients:

- 1 cup yellow split peas
- 1 small onion, diced
- 2 cloves garlic, minced
- 4 cups water or vegetable broth
- 1 tablespoon olive oil
- 1 teaspoon lemon juice
- Salt and pepper to taste

Instructions:

1. Simmer split peas, onion, garlic, and broth for 30 minutes until soft.
2. Blend or mash until smooth, then stir in olive oil, lemon juice, salt, and pepper.

Taramosalata (Fish Roe Spread)

Ingredients:

- ¼ cup tarama (fish roe)
- 1 small potato, boiled and mashed
- ½ cup olive oil
- 2 tablespoons lemon juice
- 1 clove garlic, minced

Instructions:

1. Blend tarama with mashed potato, garlic, and lemon juice.
2. Slowly drizzle in olive oil while blending until smooth.

Psari Plaki (Baked Fish with Tomatoes and Onions)

Ingredients:

- 2 fish fillets (sea bass or cod)
- 1 onion, sliced
- 2 cloves garlic, minced
- 1 cup diced tomatoes
- 1 teaspoon oregano
- 1 tablespoon olive oil
- ½ teaspoon salt
- ½ teaspoon black pepper

Instructions:

1. Sauté onions and garlic in olive oil, then add tomatoes, oregano, salt, and pepper.
2. Place fish in a baking dish and cover with tomato mixture.
3. Bake at 375°F (190°C) for 20 minutes.

Horta Vrasta (Boiled Wild Greens with Olive Oil and Lemon)

Ingredients:

- 1 bunch dandelion greens or kale
- 1 tablespoon olive oil
- Juice of 1 lemon
- Salt to taste

Instructions:

1. Boil greens for 5–7 minutes until tender.
2. Drain and toss with olive oil, lemon juice, and salt.

Xtapodi Krasato (Braised Octopus in Wine)

Ingredients:

- 1 lb octopus, cleaned and chopped
- 1 small onion, diced
- 2 cloves garlic, minced
- 1 cup red wine
- 1 can diced tomatoes
- 1 teaspoon oregano
- 1 tablespoon olive oil
- Salt and pepper to taste

Instructions:

1. Sauté onion and garlic in olive oil.
2. Add octopus, wine, tomatoes, oregano, salt, and pepper.
3. Simmer for 1 hour until tender.

Lamb Fricassee with Avgolemono Sauce

Ingredients:

- 1 lb lamb, cubed
- 2 tablespoons olive oil
- 1 onion, diced
- 2 cloves garlic, minced
- 1 cup chicken broth
- 1 cup chopped lettuce or greens
- 2 eggs
- Juice of 2 lemons

Instructions:

1. Sauté lamb, onion, and garlic in olive oil.
2. Add broth and simmer for 45 minutes.
3. Stir in greens and cook for 5 minutes.
4. Whisk eggs and lemon juice, then slowly add hot broth. Stir back into the pot.

Halva (Semolina-Based Sweet Dessert)

Ingredients:

- 1 cup semolina
- ½ cup sugar
- ½ cup olive oil
- 2 cups water
- ½ teaspoon cinnamon
- ¼ cup chopped walnuts

Instructions:

1. Heat olive oil in a pan and toast semolina until golden brown.
2. Stir in sugar, water, and cinnamon, cooking until thickened.
3. Fold in walnuts and let cool before serving.

Rizogalo (Greek Rice Pudding)

Ingredients:

- ½ cup short-grain rice
- 2 cups milk
- ¼ cup sugar
- ½ teaspoon vanilla extract
- ½ teaspoon cinnamon

Instructions:

1. Cook rice in milk over low heat until soft.
2. Stir in sugar and vanilla, simmering until thickened.
3. Garnish with cinnamon before serving.

Kourabiedes (Powdered Sugar Butter Cookies)

Ingredients:

- 1 cup butter, softened
- ½ cup powdered sugar
- 2 cups flour
- ½ teaspoon vanilla extract
- ½ cup chopped almonds
- Extra powdered sugar for dusting

Instructions:

1. Cream butter and sugar, then mix in vanilla and flour.
2. Fold in almonds and shape into small rounds.
3. Bake at 350°F (175°C) for 20 minutes.
4. Dust with powdered sugar before serving.

Kataifi (Shredded Phyllo Pastry with Nuts and Syrup)

Ingredients:

- 1 package kataifi (shredded phyllo dough)
- 1 cup mixed nuts (walnuts, almonds, pistachios), chopped
- ½ teaspoon cinnamon
- ½ cup melted butter

For Syrup:

- 1 cup sugar
- ½ cup water
- ¼ cup honey
- 1 teaspoon lemon juice

Instructions:

1. Preheat oven to 350°F (175°C).
2. Mix chopped nuts with cinnamon.
3. Take small portions of kataifi dough, place some nut mixture in the center, and roll tightly.
4. Place in a greased baking dish and brush with melted butter.
5. Bake for 35–40 minutes until golden.
6. Boil sugar, water, honey, and lemon juice for syrup, then pour over hot kataifi.

Bougatsa (Greek Custard-Filled Pastry)

Ingredients:

- 8 sheets phyllo dough
- 2 cups milk
- ½ cup sugar
- ¼ cup semolina
- 1 teaspoon vanilla extract
- 2 eggs
- ¼ cup melted butter
- Powdered sugar and cinnamon for garnish

Instructions:

1. Heat milk and slowly stir in semolina and sugar until thick.
2. Remove from heat, mix in vanilla and beaten eggs.
3. Layer phyllo sheets, brushing each with butter, and pour custard inside.
4. Fold and bake at 375°F (190°C) for 30 minutes.
5. Dust with powdered sugar and cinnamon before serving.

Loukaniko (Greek Sausage with Orange Zest)

Ingredients:

- 1 lb ground pork
- 1 clove garlic, minced
- 1 teaspoon fennel seeds
- 1 teaspoon dried oregano
- ½ teaspoon black pepper
- 1 teaspoon grated orange zest
- 1 teaspoon salt

Instructions:

1. Mix all ingredients and shape into sausages.
2. Let rest for a few hours or overnight.
3. Grill or pan-fry until cooked through.

Soutzoukakia (Greek Meatballs in Tomato Sauce)

Ingredients:

- 1 lb ground beef
- 1 small onion, minced
- 2 cloves garlic, minced
- ½ cup breadcrumbs
- 1 egg
- 1 teaspoon cumin
- ½ teaspoon cinnamon
- 1 can tomato sauce
- 1 tablespoon olive oil

Instructions:

1. Mix beef, onion, garlic, breadcrumbs, egg, cumin, and cinnamon.
2. Shape into oval meatballs and pan-fry in olive oil.
3. Add tomato sauce and simmer for 20 minutes.

Choriatiki Omeleta (Greek Village Omelet)

Ingredients:

- 3 eggs
- ½ cup feta cheese, crumbled
- ½ cup diced tomatoes
- ¼ cup sliced olives
- 1 teaspoon olive oil
- ½ teaspoon oregano

Instructions:

1. Whisk eggs and cook in olive oil.
2. Add feta, tomatoes, and olives.
3. Sprinkle with oregano and fold over.

Lagana (Greek Flatbread)

Ingredients:

- 3 cups all-purpose flour
- 1 teaspoon salt
- 1 teaspoon sugar
- 1 teaspoon yeast
- 1 cup warm water
- 2 tablespoons olive oil
- 2 tablespoons sesame seeds

Instructions:

1. Mix flour, salt, sugar, yeast, and warm water to form dough.
2. Let rise for 1 hour.
3. Roll out into an oval, brush with olive oil, and sprinkle with sesame seeds.
4. Bake at 375°F (190°C) for 25 minutes.

Tsoureki (Greek Easter Bread)

Ingredients:

- 3 ½ cups flour
- 1 teaspoon salt
- ½ cup sugar
- 1 tablespoon yeast
- ½ cup warm milk
- 2 eggs
- ¼ cup melted butter
- 1 teaspoon mahleb (optional)
- 1 teaspoon orange zest

Instructions:

1. Mix flour, salt, sugar, yeast, and warm milk.
2. Add eggs, butter, mahleb, and orange zest. Knead into dough.
3. Let rise for 1 hour, then shape into a braid.
4. Bake at 350°F (175°C) for 30 minutes.

Pita Me Gyro (Greek Gyro Wrap)

Ingredients:

- 2 pita breads
- ½ lb cooked gyro meat (chicken, lamb, or pork)
- ½ cup tzatziki sauce
- ½ cup sliced tomatoes
- ½ cup sliced onions
- ¼ cup lettuce

Instructions:

1. Warm pita bread.
2. Layer with gyro meat, tzatziki, tomatoes, onions, and lettuce.
3. Roll and serve.

Sfakiani Pita (Cheese-Filled Cretan Pie with Honey)

Ingredients:

- 1 cup flour
- ½ teaspoon salt
- ½ teaspoon sugar
- ½ cup water
- ½ cup ricotta or mizithra cheese
- 1 tablespoon honey

Instructions:

1. Mix flour, salt, sugar, and water into dough.
2. Roll out and fill with cheese, sealing edges.
3. Pan-fry until golden brown and drizzle with honey.

Kalamarakia Tiganita (Fried Calamari)

Ingredients:

- ½ lb squid, cleaned and sliced
- ½ cup flour
- ½ teaspoon salt
- ½ teaspoon black pepper
- Oil for frying
- Lemon wedges for serving

Instructions:

1. Toss squid in flour, salt, and pepper.
2. Fry in hot oil for 2–3 minutes until golden brown.
3. Serve with lemon wedges.

Midia Saganaki (Mussels in Tomato and Feta Sauce)

Ingredients:

- 1 lb mussels, cleaned
- 1 small onion, diced
- 2 cloves garlic, minced
- 1 cup diced tomatoes
- ½ cup white wine
- ¼ teaspoon red pepper flakes
- ¼ cup crumbled feta cheese
- 1 tablespoon olive oil

Instructions:

1. Sauté onion and garlic in olive oil.
2. Add tomatoes, wine, and red pepper flakes. Simmer for 5 minutes.
3. Add mussels, cover, and cook until they open.
4. Sprinkle with feta before serving.

Amygdalota (Greek Almond Cookies)

Ingredients:

- 2 cups almond flour
- ½ cup sugar
- 2 egg whites
- ½ teaspoon almond extract
- ¼ cup sliced almonds (for garnish)
- Powdered sugar (for dusting)

Instructions:

1. Preheat oven to 350°F (175°C).
2. Mix almond flour, sugar, egg whites, and almond extract into a dough.
3. Shape into small balls and place on a baking sheet.
4. Press sliced almonds on top.
5. Bake for 15 minutes, then dust with powdered sugar.

Spetsofai (Sausage and Peppers in Tomato Sauce)

Ingredients:

- 1 lb Greek sausage (or chorizo), sliced
- 1 red bell pepper, sliced
- 1 green bell pepper, sliced
- 1 small onion, chopped
- 2 cloves garlic, minced
- 1 can diced tomatoes
- 1 teaspoon oregano
- 1 teaspoon paprika
- 1 tablespoon olive oil

Instructions:

1. Heat olive oil in a pan and sauté sausage until browned.
2. Add onions, garlic, and bell peppers. Cook for 5 minutes.
3. Stir in tomatoes, oregano, and paprika. Simmer for 20 minutes.

Hortopita (Wild Greens and Cheese Pie)

Ingredients:

- 1 lb mixed wild greens (dandelion, spinach, or chard), chopped
- 1 small onion, diced
- 2 cloves garlic, minced
- 1 cup feta cheese, crumbled
- 2 eggs, beaten
- 8 sheets phyllo dough
- ¼ cup melted butter
- 1 teaspoon dill
- ½ teaspoon black pepper

Instructions:

1. Sauté onion, garlic, and greens until wilted.
2. Mix with feta, eggs, dill, and pepper.
3. Layer phyllo sheets in a greased baking dish, brushing each with butter.
4. Add filling, top with more phyllo, and bake at 375°F (190°C) for 30 minutes.

Paximadia (Greek Twice-Baked Biscotti)

Ingredients:

- 2 cups all-purpose flour
- ½ cup sugar
- ½ teaspoon cinnamon
- ½ teaspoon baking powder
- ½ cup almonds, chopped
- ½ cup olive oil
- ¼ cup orange juice

Instructions:

1. Preheat oven to 350°F (175°C).
2. Mix flour, sugar, cinnamon, baking powder, and almonds.
3. Add olive oil and orange juice, mixing into a dough.
4. Shape into a log and bake for 25 minutes.
5. Slice into biscotti and bake for another 10 minutes until crispy.

Fasolakia Ladera (Braised Green Beans in Olive Oil)

Ingredients:

- 1 lb green beans, trimmed
- 1 small onion, diced
- 2 cloves garlic, minced
- 1 can diced tomatoes
- ½ teaspoon oregano
- ½ teaspoon cinnamon
- ¼ cup olive oil
- Salt and pepper to taste

Instructions:

1. Heat olive oil in a pot and sauté onion and garlic.
2. Add green beans, tomatoes, oregano, cinnamon, salt, and pepper.
3. Simmer for 30 minutes until beans are tender.

Marides Tiganites (Fried Whitebait Fish)

Ingredients:

- ½ lb whitebait fish, cleaned
- ½ cup flour
- ½ teaspoon salt
- ½ teaspoon black pepper
- Oil for frying
- Lemon wedges for serving

Instructions:

1. Toss fish in flour, salt, and pepper.
2. Fry in hot oil for 2–3 minutes until golden brown.
3. Serve with lemon wedges.

Galaktoboureko (Greek Custard Pie with Syrup)

Ingredients:

- 8 sheets phyllo dough
- 4 cups milk
- ½ cup semolina
- ½ cup sugar
- 3 eggs
- 1 teaspoon vanilla extract
- ¼ cup melted butter

For Syrup:

- 1 cup sugar
- ½ cup water
- ¼ cup honey
- 1 teaspoon lemon juice

Instructions:

1. Heat milk and semolina, stirring until thick.
2. Whisk in sugar, eggs, and vanilla.
3. Layer phyllo sheets in a greased baking dish, brushing with butter.
4. Pour custard inside, fold over phyllo, and bake at 375°F (190°C) for 35 minutes.
5. Boil sugar, water, honey, and lemon juice for syrup, then pour over hot pie.